# VOLUME 2

THE HIDDEN GODDESS WITH A TWISTED MIND

BY
JONIECE JACKSON

Text Copyright © Joniece Jackson 2017. All rights reserved. This book or parts thereof may not be reproduced in any form, stored in any retrieval system, or transmitted in any form by any means—electronic, mechanical, photocopy, recording, or otherwise—without prior written permission of the publisher, except as provided by United States of America copyright law.

## ***DEDICATION***

Thank you for reading my twisted mind.

V2 was written just for you,
And many other supporters that's been waiting.
.

## *PREFACE*

Each book is put in order to tell not only her story,

but what thousands of others readers have experienced in

abuse, violence, feeling lost,

And finding self.

This book dances with feelings and twirls with words to keep you engaged, entertained,

and on your toes.

Welcome to V2

## Table of Contents

| | |
|---|---|
| *Dedication* | 3 |
| *Preface* | 4 |
| *Dear Grandma* | 7 |
| *Am I the caged bird?* | 14 |
| *The Life Of Poet* | 17 |
| *The Battle Isn't Over* | 20 |
| *Why Me?* | 28 |
| *Not Today Satan* | 31 |
| *I Got me* | 39 |
| *I'm not heartless,* | 44 |
| *That One Ex* | 50 |
| *When a poet is in love* | 55 |
| *My Savage Side* | 60 |
| *She deserves Better* | 66 |
| *I Love ThAT Woman* | 70 |
| *I thought you loved me.* | 74 |
| *Not like you* | 76 |
| *Jump* | 81 |
| *Are you?* | 83 |
| *Did You?* | 86 |
| *Who are you?* | 89 |
| *Hey. . . .* | 94 |
| *Everything I Touch Dies.. . .* | 96 |

***What It Means To Make Love***                101
***Dear Future Husband***                        103

### ***DEAR GRANDMA***

There isn't a day that goes by
when you're not on my mind,
And I
Still

miss

you.
Can you see me up there?

.

I swear,
I'm doing the best that I can.

.

I get paid to write,

Coped feelings with pens.

.

.

You were right when you told me,

"Everyone's not your friend"

.

Well Grandma,
This year,
Betrayal is a trend.

I miss you.

.

The pillows you've made me still rests my head.

.

The blankets will stay even after I wed.

.

Your spirit still dance,
though your body is dead.

.

And when the holidays come,
the tears still shed.

.

I
Miss
you.

.

Grandma,
I kept your bible.
and read a verse everyday.

.

Taught myself his word
and even learned how to pray.

I'm far from perfect,
and still quite the sinner.

But I like to thank God for every simple dinner.

.

I miss you.

Can you see me up there?

.

.

.

The brightest star is when you wink.
I know it's you that turns skies pink.
I say less words the more I think,

But you can't hear them
So I drink.

.
.
.

And I
still remember your last month of life.
．

You lost to Cancer,

and it left us in strife.
．
．
A loving mother and a beautiful wife
．
．
Got the best gift of all,

Eternal life
．

．

．

．
I miss you.

They put you in the ground
despite of your wishes.

.

I think about it now
as I'm washing dishes.

.

You said,

"I don't want no stinking bugs crawling
on my body"

And we laughed about it then
but now my nose is kinda snotty.

.
.
.
.

But I miss you.

Can you see me up there?

.

I asked God why, but he didn't answer.

And after the pain my name was then slandered.

.

I still don't fit in,

I'm not even standard,

.

.

But my backhand is stronger

.

.

.

as if I'm a pander.

### *<u>AM I THE CAGED BIRD?</u>*

I'm surrounded by walls
Locked away with no key.

Is it locked from the inside?
.
Am I afraid?
.
Is it me?
.
.

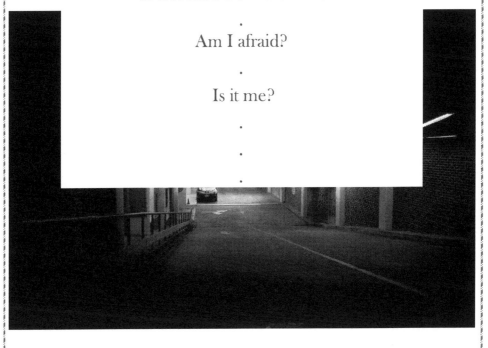

I guess it's not all bad,

.

I got loud

.

But am I free?

.

.

.

Maya said a cage bird,

.

.

.

Did she know
I would sing?

### ***THE LIFE OF POET***

Poets experience life differently.

.

We feel more,
We fall harder
and cry longer.

.

We channel what's left of us into our words.

.

Scramble up new pieces
for fresh cuts and old wounds,
to only be broken once more.

.

And we do this over and over again.

.

Maybe its social insanity,

We're dressed in dope rhymes
With bedazzled profanity.

.

Stripped from high words
and dusted in vanity

.

Don't call it a cult,
It's Christianity.

We paint with our words
and give feelings color,

We hurt for the next
and love like a mother.
.
Give peace to the mind
Like we're running from time
Don't step inside mine
'cause most don't survive

From the darkness and heartaches
That makes me fucking thrive.
,
.
.
We were made for this.
.
.
.

But then again
it could just be me.

.

I'm just the girl that feels sorta weak.

.

like Tinkerbell to Peter,

.

can't fly without belief,

.

But cries herself to sleep

.

like
sad songs on repeat

.

like deep quotes you retweet.

.

.

A Poets Life: You see me?

### ***THE BATTLE ISN'T OVER***

I fight a lot of demons
Every
Single
day.

.

I struggle to let go of the past.
I struggle to forgive and play.

.

I struggle to open up,
and I struggle to even trust.

.

Shit, I struggle to live,
And that one's a fucking must!

.

If you're reading my books
you'll see a few stories why!

I'm sorry,

I don't always shit sprinkles and butterflies.

I've been hurt.

I've been broken.
Used and Abused.

I've been damaged and tossed.

And my soul is still bruised.
.

.

.

I talk to God everyday
to help me heal.

.

Licked the glue at the top just to seal the deal.

.

Sent it off in the mail just to stay concealed

.

But sometimes I miss shots,
Like Shaquille O Neil.

.

.

To trust again is very ideal.

## MATTHEW FOUR THIRTY NINE
Said "Peace! Be Still"

Wind blowing rhymes that feels unreal.
But I'm just trynna eat

And make a man a good meal.

Put the rest up in the fridge,

and I want stainless steel!

To be surrounded by people
	that love me for me.

.

People with a vision
without hidden fees.

.

I don't know what that's like,
But I do trust in thee.

.

He always has a plan,

.

I mean,
He created me . .

.

.

I won't go far on my own,
So In God I Trust.

.

That's coming from the girl
That kneed to chest to the bus.

.

I took a lot of L's and bounced back,
So that's always a plus.

.

But It sucks,

.

.

.

.

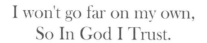

I've been so fucked up
that it fears me to try to reach out.
.
Is that me having pride
.
or me
and self doubt?
.
.
I can't really lie,
my phone lives in a drought.
.

the only messages I had
said "past due accounts"
.
.

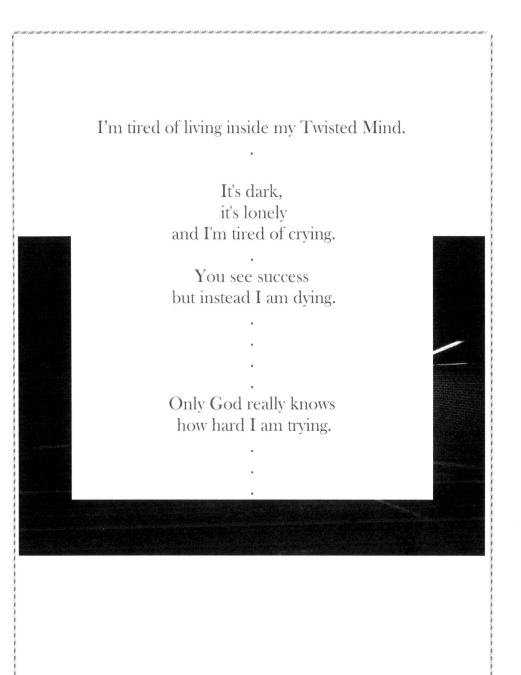

I'm tired of living inside my Twisted Mind.

.

It's dark,
it's lonely
and I'm tired of crying.

.

You see success
but instead I am dying.

.

.

.

Only God really knows
how hard I am trying.

.

.

### ***WHY ME?***

God, why did have to you make me a writer?

.

.

"Cause people like you
are the strongest of fighters"

.

.

But what if I pop like a wheel on a tire?

.

.

.

"What if you catch all your heart desires?"

.

.

God, I'm not really sure
why you made me a poet.

.

.

.

"You can move mountains with pens
and you know it"

.

.

But what if fail, God?

.

.

What if I blow it?

.

.

.

"Just Channel your pain,
then flow it and show it"

.

God, why do I have to feel all this pain?

.

.

.

"Cause I'll cure your heart
when you call on my name"

.

.

But what if the devil don't want me to go?

.

.

"You are my child, Keep using your glow"

### *<u>NOT TODAY SATAN</u>*

The devil likes to paint me pictures
that those that embrace ignorance and misery,

.

Are the only ones that get put down in history.

.

.

He whispers in my ear
opens a box full of trickery,

.

.

But I can't really lie.

.

It does
look
so
shimmery.

.

.

.

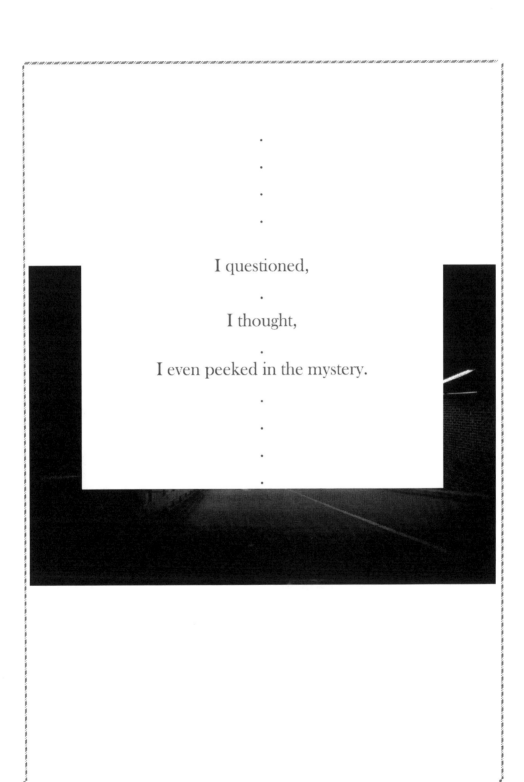

.
.
.
.

I questioned,

.

I thought,

.

I even peeked in the mystery.

.

.

.

Such sin

.

.

so close

.

So far in proximity.

.

But the devil's a lie,

.

"The Good Sin"
- Contradictory

.

.

But I threw that part in just as an auxiliary.

.

He tells me they will love me

.

if I just do one line.

.

But God gave me a gift,
And said

.

"Yo put it in a rhyme."

.

Blessing will always come

.

but it's all on Heaven's time.

.

And when I chat it up with Him
I know that I'll do fine,

.

.

But,

The devil is dangling a carrot in my face.

.

They say success is not a race,

.

But what if I
move from fucking base

.

And I can't keep up the pace

.

Then all my moves will be retraced,

And all my dreams will replaced.

.

.

.

.

The devil had tried to steal my own little heart.

．

He gave me false love
cause it's my soul that can't be bought.

．

Dropped me out of school,
Cause Self-Made just wasn't taught.

．

But you don't want real,

Just love of the thought.

．
．
．
．

Ignorance and Misery,

that's how the devil thrives.

But little do they know

that it's strongest that survives.

### *I GOT ME*

No one got me like I got myself,

But God.

.

No one loves me as much as I do,

.

If they say,

then it's fraud.

.

No one understands me,

I don't expect them too neither.

.

But here's my life

See what I go through Readers.

.

It's me against the world,

Like It has always been.

.

My dad doesn't love me ,

.

I have no friends,

.

The realest nigga on my team

is just a black pen,

.

But I'm a lot stronger now

than I was back then.

.

.

They kicked me low,

Rubbed my face in the dirt,

.

I wear my heart on my sleeve

so you see how I hurt.

.

Them dudes ain't love me,

just loved what's under my skirt.

.

Until I wised up

and demanded my ring first.

.

.

I hear hoes are winning

but that's coming from thots.

.

If you ain't chasing money,

you ain't shooting a shot.

.

Bastard running to the dreams

like hands on a clock,

Next move pulling up like its Drake to The Dot.

.

.

.

You may think you know me

but I'm the Queen of Unknown.

.

With a thrown that's made of lost dreams,

blood

and bones.

.

.

.

### ***I'M NOT HEARTLESS,***
I'm just protected.

.

It still beats for little things;

.

Just not for sex with no rings

.

And loose strings with mood swings.

.

.

.

I'm not heartless

.

I'm just player 2.

.

Just happens I spit better game
Than what most think they threw.

.

.

.

I'm not heartless
.
I can love.
.
I can give you peace,
.
I can wash your pain with doves
Your heart will skip a beat
.
.
.

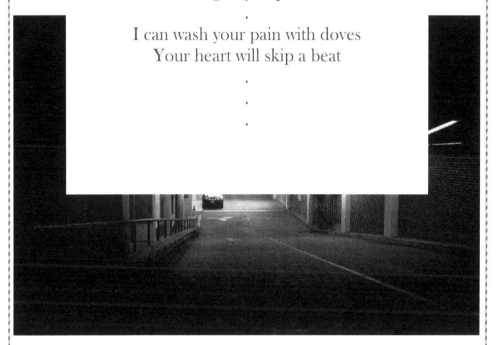

.
I swear I'm not cold,
.
I'm just not warmed up.
.
It gets really old
to keep falling for fuckups
.
That's stuck to the cycle of breaking hearts,
.
Playing like children
And claiming they're grownups.
.
.
.
.
.

I'm not heartless,
.
In fact mine is made of gold.
.
24K but a rare one that don't fold.
.
.
.

I'm not perfect by any fucking means.
.
I'm not the pretty girl
you see on big screens,
.
I'm not like the "bad bitch"
that you'll post in your memes
.
But one thing I am
.
Is one hell of a Queen.
.
.
.

if you don't think I'm worth it,

Then we was never meant to be,

Cause I know **MY KING**

will get down on one knee.

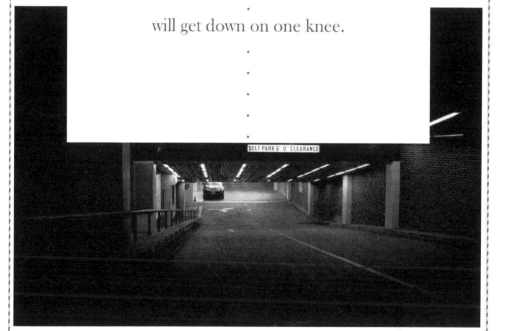

### *That One Ex*

Someone once told me that

I would never find better

if I was to move on from him.

He would say things like

the next guy would beat me

And will never be better than him.

"I'm not like your ex"

"You know I'm the best"

And every moment with him was like

Clocks to a test,

Timing my answers for his satisfaction,

Shutting me down,

Reverse manifesting

So I closed that last chapter,

And now I lay resting

Though it was him

that stayed fucking sexting

To everyone else

But me.

I was the woman that rubbed on his feet,

And foolish for me

cause I loved with no ring

But some reason my head said

"Forever will be"

And that was the Devil

Stealing from me,

Cause God never said that.

And my God's not a liar.

He held to my hand

when I walked through fire.

He is my friend like on Lizzie McGruire.

.

Sending me clues,

.

Like Kima -- The Wire

Someone really told me I will never find better.

But one man's trash

is another man's treasure.

### ***WHEN A POET IS IN LOVE***

You become their rhythm and blues

.

Like alcoholics to their booze,

.

Like designer shoes to Jimmy Choos,

.

Like Steve on drugs when Blue gave Clues,

.

Like wet to water,
But a live in cruise.

.

.

.

.

It makes me see sick
I can be slick

.

Like Ice in the freezer.

.

but you ain't wanna believe her

.

you tickled and teased her

.

And all just to please her,

.

And now you are here,

.

with a poet in love.

.

.

You touched her heart without wearing a glove....
You gave her

S.urrealistic

.

T.hought

.

D.esires!

.

.

Like Gator boats in 2002 on #BigTymers

.

.

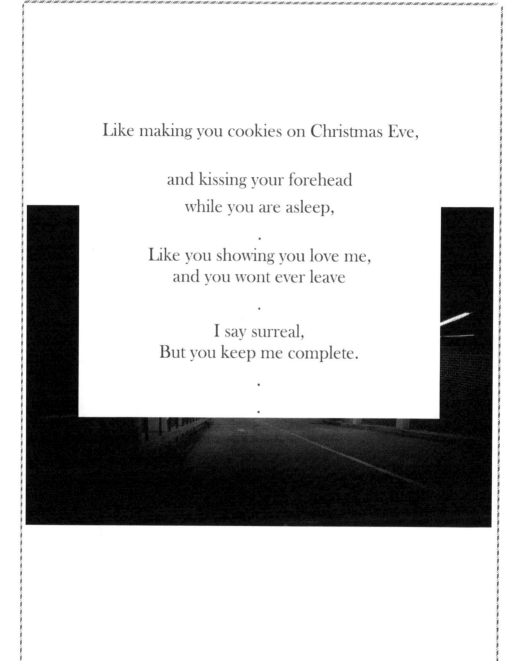

Like making you cookies on Christmas Eve,

and kissing your forehead
while you are asleep,

.

Like you showing you love me,
and you wont ever leave

.

I say surreal,
But you keep me complete.

.

.

When a poet's in love,
this is what you get.

.

.

Hand written rhymes

.

.

that you'll never forget.

### ***MY SAVAGE SIDE***

My savage side is saying
start pulling daddies and uncles.

.

Most dudes my age
like dropping women and fumble.

.

When it's the real women
that'll ride through the jungle.

.

But they'll chase a "bad bitch"
and forget to stay humble.

.

.

.

This generation done killed love,

.

How the fuck did that crumble?

.

When my peoples were coming up
it was ten toes before a struggle.

.

They had each other back,
And fought through all of their troubles.

.

Hustled their own pieces
And put together a puzzle.

.

.

.

But this generation
just don't know
what
love
is.

.

They'll run at the first sign of any
issues and frizz,

.

Play dumb to easy questions
and fail the pop quiz

.

Admire false love,
Remember Amber and Wiz?

.

.

.

My savage side is saying
Just go handle your bizz.

.

But everyone needs
someone to share that bag with,

.

Build the empire
and pass it on to the kids.

.

You say you want loud
but yet you settle for mids.

.

.

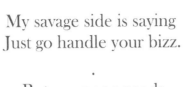

This generation done fucked up loyalty.
Acting like peasants
but screaming out royalty.

Search for fake titles
and forget to seek buoyancy.

.

Full of shit actors,
Watch out for the toiletry

.

.

My savage side is saying,
Don't be a good a girl.

.

All the hoes are winning
All the diamonds and pearls

.

But
my God told me,
"Stay Strong, Cause I heard"

.

"Wait for the man that studies my word"

.

There's more in the spring
Than the bees and the birds.

.

In between notes like the music and its thirds.

### ***SHE DESERVES BETTER***

.

She deserves handwritten love letters.

.

She deserves to be held

and

wrapped in your sweater

.

She deserves to be treated

like the first time you met her.

.

Are you paying attention?

Cause this shit is real clever. .

.

Treat her like you love her and watch it get wetter

She deserves to know when she's on your mind.

.

She deserves a real date

that you planned and designed.

.

She deserves to be loved,

Not broken and undermined

.

She deserves an ate pussy

and a sweet glass of wine

.

.

You got that?

.

.

She deserves to smile and laugh till she cries.

·

She deserves you to be there

to wipe tears from her eyes.

·

She deserves to be held,

and never let go.

·

She deserves forehead kisses

and soft tickled toes.

·

·

She deserves to be treated

like the Queen that she is.

·

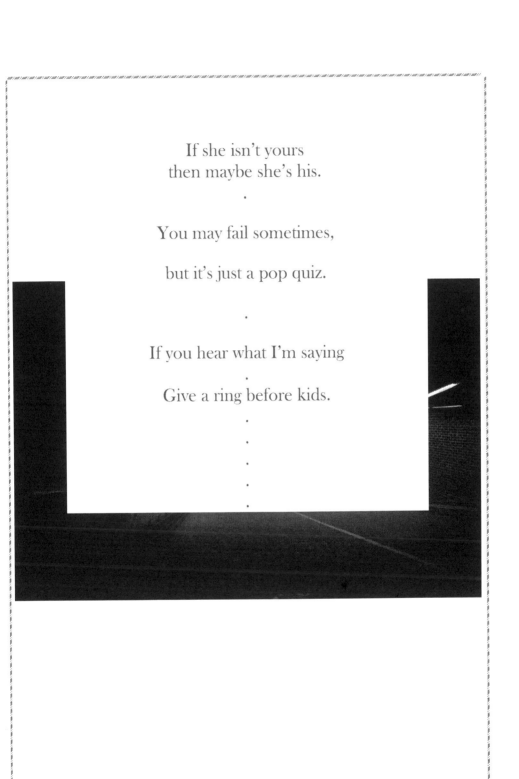

### *<u>I LOVE THAT WOMAN</u>*

I love the woman
that I'm becoming.

.

Though my paths'
been very humbling.

.

Fumbling and rumbling
Tumbling and all.

.

4 foot 10,
But I bark like I'm tall.

.

.

I love the woman I see in the mirror,

Since smokescreen passed
I can see even clearer.

The reflection of me is never more dearer,

You gotta love you
so you won't live so bitter.

.

.

.

.

The hate and salt is just extra sauce,

The truth I speak
but it's shade you toss.
.
At the end of the day it's you at a lost.
.
And I'm still smiling
but it was I that got crossed.
.
.

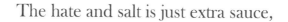

Letters and words,
My gift apparatus.

·

The only flaw you may yell is
maybe my fatness.

·

But I can drop that,
Then you

·

And smoke a blunt while I'm at it.

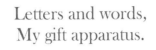

### *<u>I THOUGHT YOU LOVED ME.</u>*

Yet you never said that.

.

You just did things to "beat up my cat".

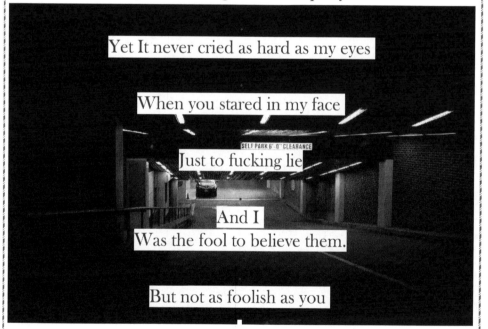

Yet It never cried as hard as my eyes

When you stared in my face

Just to fucking lie

And I
Was the fool to believe them.

But not as foolish as you

.

Who dropped a gem.

.

.

### ***NOT LIKE YOU***

I don't think I can love anyone else
the way I loved you.
But maybe in another life
you'll find me again.

.

You made my heart skip
like ink in a dried out pen.
And I never wanted to stop being friends,
But you know what they say,

.

Good things come to an end.

.

I never cared what you did or didn't have.
It was the time you gave me that made me glad,
And the way you craved me even when I was sad,
And what I felt for you
was more than a fab.

.

I don't think I can love anyone else
The way I loved you.

.

Pretty fucked up for me
because I don't really want to.

.

Cause it'll end just like this,

.

A warm heart to cold blue

.

Shit, a few men want me
and I'm here writing about you.

.

Look, I'm a poet.
You knew this is what I'd do.

.

Let love take me and make me a fool.

.

Sometimes I bite more than what I can chew:

But the spark that ignited me
was all because of you.

.

You shouldn't lose a 80 for 20
when you look like an Andrew.

I thought I was your 90
I had stopped counting to.

.

It was that night
that my eyes had met you.

.

.

.

.

And It's sad, ya know?

.

.

.

This world today only care about hoes.
When there's good people out here
that'll love you head to toe.

.

But that's some real shit
that just happened to flow.
Just read the next stanza

.

Okay, ready?

.

.

.

.

Go!

I don't think I can love anyone else
the way that I loved you.
So I'll give it back to me,
And talk to God about you.

.

And to any man that's reading this status,
Don't hurt the good girls.

.

Just take her hand in marriage.

.

There's no Queen out here
That deserves this kind of damage.

That's how you create the women
with emotional baggage.

.

.

.

### ***JUMP***

I cry with my words
when my eyes want to weep.

.

I smile at random people,
And they stare and won't speak.

.

I want to save the world,
But no one can save me.

.

I'm still asking God
What he wants me to be.

.

My knees like to tremble,
And my body feels weak.

.

When I fall, I'm alone
There's no one to catch me.

.

My mind feels trapped,
But I want to be free.

.


.

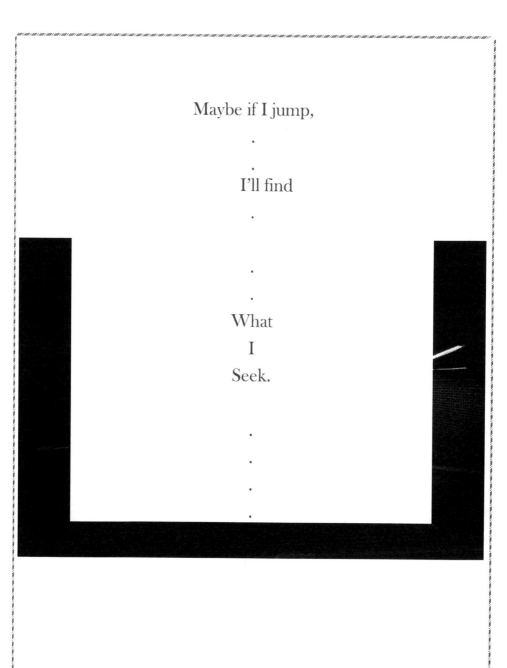

## ***ARE YOU?***

Are you proud of me now?
They're chanting my name.

You've always believed
I wouldn't have any fame.

You glanced at my words
And paused them like a game

But it was I that had won
I guess it's you that got played.
.
.
.
.
.

Are you proud of me now?
I now own my own.

A place to call home
And a place with my throne.

Are you proud of me now?
I got that degree.

I only did it for you
But I kept that low-key

.
.
.
.

Are you proud of me now?

Did I make you grin?

You thought my life was sin
.
Now I'm paid to use pens.

Are you proud of me now?
.
.
'Cause I sure am.

## ***DID YOU?***

Did you think of me
when my first heartbeat appeared?

.

Were you stirred from reality?
Disbelieved in causality
That I
Could be
Yours?

.

Did you think about those sores?

.

Score years to decide to love what is yours.

.
.
.

Did you care that you've missed my first step . .

And everyone after that
Yet
You say you want me in your life,
But actions speaks facts.

.
.
.
.

Do you see her when you look at me?

You see how you ran from your responsibility.

How you created this monster,
This beast that's breathes within me.

.
.
.

Did you know that I was your own?

That your blood streams through my finger tips
to my toes,
But how I've never seen you at any of my shows.
.
.
.

Did you really think that I didn't know?
.
.

Now that I glow
You stand before me to get some shine.

Now you want some of mine,
With no exceptions of decline.

But did you think of me?
.
.
.
.

### ***WHO ARE YOU?***

I look at you and wonder who you are.

What happened?
and
how'd you get this far?
.

You were just a lost soul
that was wishing on stars,

You were just inhaling your weed
and dancing on mars.
But,
when I look at you,
I can see your scars.
.
.
.
.
.

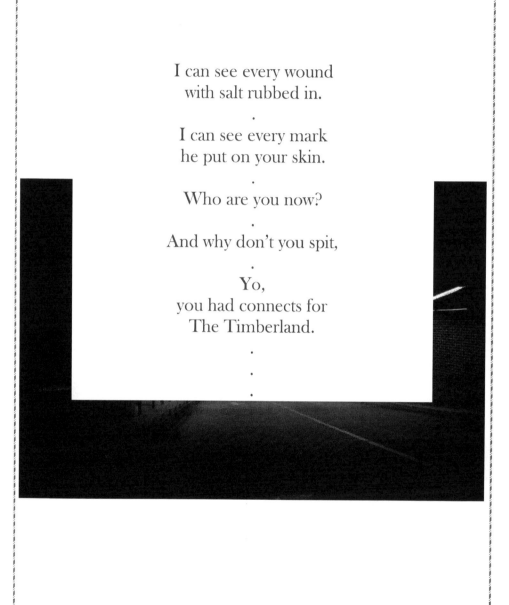

I can see every wound
with salt rubbed in.

.

I can see every mark
he put on your skin.

.

Who are you now?

.

And why don't you spit,

.

Yo,
you had connects for
The Timberland.

.
.
.

I can see your fears.
And how they turn into tears
And Miss
Chugging the beers won't wine back the years,

.

But,
You have your billion
And all checks were fucking cleared.
So,
Who are you now?
My love
My dear.

.
.
.

What happened to you?
Did you forget how to write?

.

Did you throw it away?
Did they turn down your light?

.
.
.
.

Your mind had snapped
like an acoustic guitar string
you dabbled with areopleustics
but flew higher than they.

.

You injected cabernet into your blood stream
Got your 9 to 5
And forgot your fucking dream.

.

Who are you my love?
And where's the fucking team?

.

I know you're fucking tired,
We can hear it in your screams,
We want to see you win,
Get the bag by any means.

.

Dreams turn to reality,
Faster than what it seems.

## *HEY. . . .*

I'm Joniece
and I have a problem.

A couple of them
if you have time to listen.

You see,
I talk to God
and I say I'm Christian.

But that's the same effectiveness
as a broken condom.
But I live in peace
and they folds like wontons.

In case you were wondering,
It's pronounced "John-Niece".

And I'm not a "Hood bitch"
But I lived on the east.

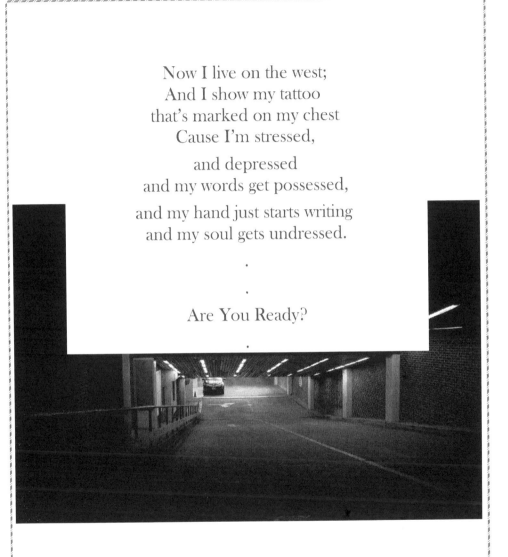

Now I live on the west;
And I show my tattoo
that's marked on my chest
Cause I'm stressed,

and depressed
and my words get possessed,

and my hand just starts writing
and my soul gets undressed.

.
.

Are You Ready?

.

### *EVERYTHING I TOUCH DIES....*

Do you know what that's like?
To have the passion to make things grow,
To prosper from head to toe,
And it does the opposite,
No matter the energy that's deposited?

Everything I want leaves.
Do you know what that's like?
The person of your dreams believes that
You are not good enough like she or he
But you cry and plead so they won't leave,
And they do just that,
with a broken heart left on your sleeve.

Do you know what it's like?

Everyone I love, hates.
Do you know what that's like?
To love other people with different traits,
See some were great friends,

and others were dates,

You sat at a table to play crazy eights,

Uno, checkers or even spades,

You give them your love

but it's you that gets played.

Do you know what it's like?

Do you know what it's like
To be born to die but expected to fight

with all your might

to fill the exception of someone else,

Cause if you live for yourself
you'll get hit with thick belts,

Strike fear in your heart to stay in line,

To be someone else that they've designed,

And 20 years later

don't want you to shine.

Do you know what it's like?

Do you know what it's like to cry yourself sleep?

.

Hold the pillow to your face just
so no one will hear you weep.

But their counting on the day to post

"I hope you

Rest

In

Peace"

But no one wants to help you
when your soul is at defeat.
.
Do you know what it's like?

Do you know what it's like
To set fire to a rose?

.

It's like beauty in the struggle,
Pen to paper, I suppose.

Will I ever make it?

No one cares,

No one knows.

But they'll hit the like button,

And enjoy the fucking show.

Do you know what its like?

### ***WHAT IT MEANS TO MAKE LOVE***

I want you to make love to my mind
And reproduce
an unforgettable experience:
set
my
soul
on
fire.
Make my thoughts shake in your arms
And caress them with yours.

Touch me with no hands
Taste me with your eyes
Lick
My
Heart
Till love comes.

Bite my insecurities and
Suck
On
My
Faith

Break down my walls.

Did you catch that?

Will you catch me?

.Why only score a few points,
when you can have the trophy?

## *DEAR FUTURE HUSBAND*

My dearest Black King;
I'm waiting for you.

And I'm so excited to show you
how much I love you.
—How much I need you.

I can play the "strong" girl
till I'm blue in the face

but I am not complete without you
— I came from your rib
and put up a good chase.

You must be incomplete too,
And if only you knew the things I will do,
When you let me fill you,
So we can be whole.

The world is so cold,
But my heart is still gold,
Let me keep you warm,
So our lives can unfold.

.

Let our minds dance together under the stars.
Let our souls become one.

.

Let me be your loving wife,
And awesome mother to our son.

.

Have patience with me,

my love.

.

I searched for you and failed.
You see

Fools aren't Kings

so of course they all bailed.
And I'm sorry
— I should have waited longer.

.

No one can wear your shoes.
And all the fucking bullshit just left me

lost and confused
and heart slightly bruised.
And I'm scared.
I'm terrified
I'm trembling in my boats,
But I have faith in God
that he will bring me to you.

.

Or

you to me.

.

Whatever our story is supposed to be.
But I'm going to love you,
The same way I love me.

.

I'm waiting for you.
Love,
Your Bride To Be.